LIVE AT THE HOLLYWOOD BOWL

A RON HOWARD FILM
EIGHT DAYS A WEEK
THE TOURING YEARS

Cover image © Bob Bonis Archive

"Roll Over Beethoven" omitted due to licensing restrictions

ISBN 978-1-4950-8076-0

HAL•LEONARD®

7777 W. BLUEMOUND RD. P.O. BOX 13819 MILWAUKEE, WI 53213

Visit Hal Leonard Online at
www.halleonard.com

TWIST AND SHOUT

Words and Music by BERT RUSSELL
and PHIL MEDLEY

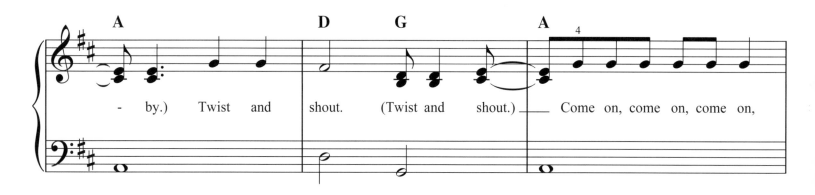

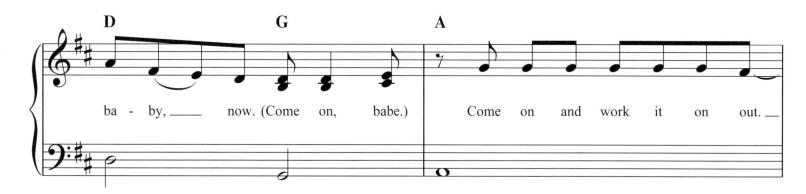

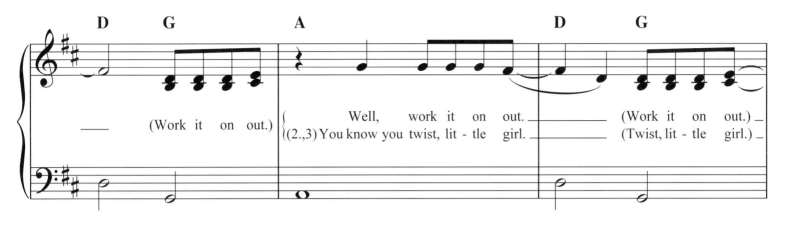

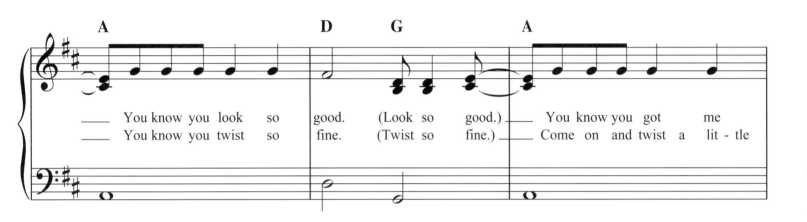

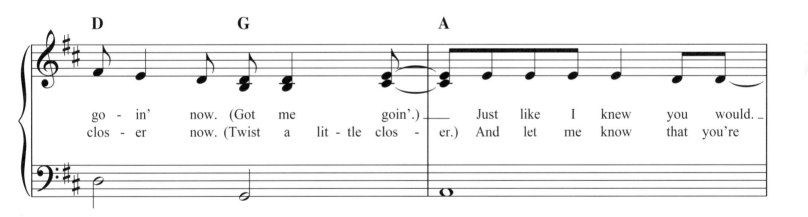

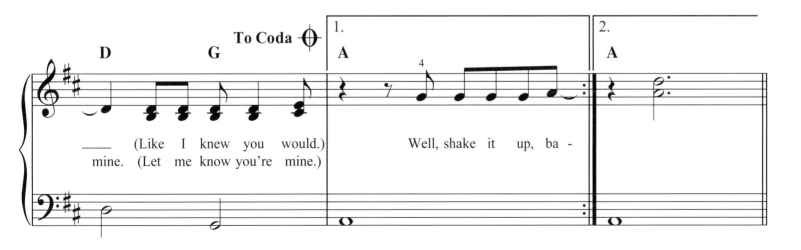

4

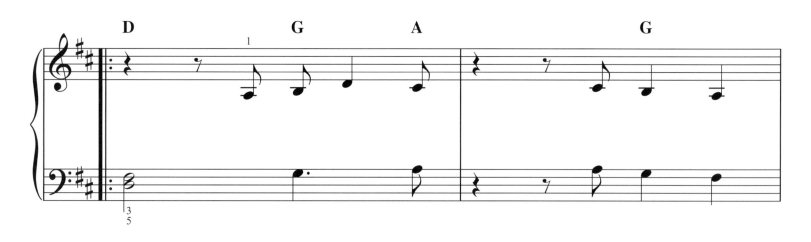

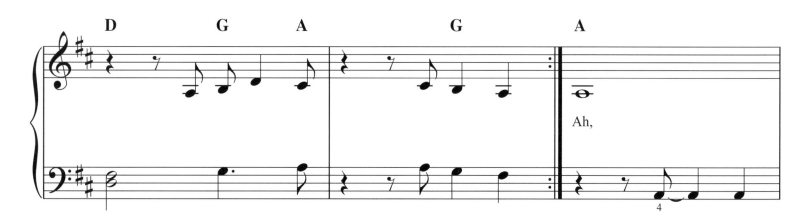

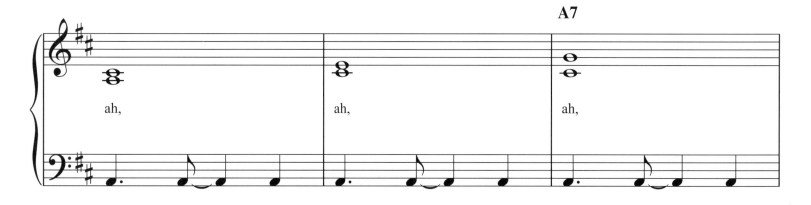

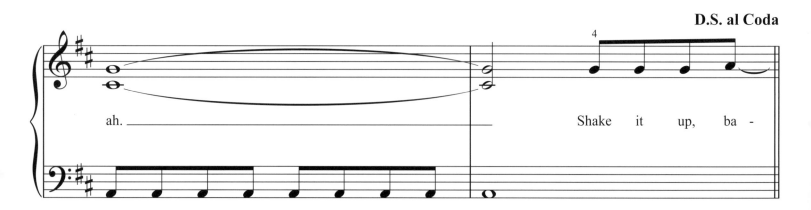

CODA

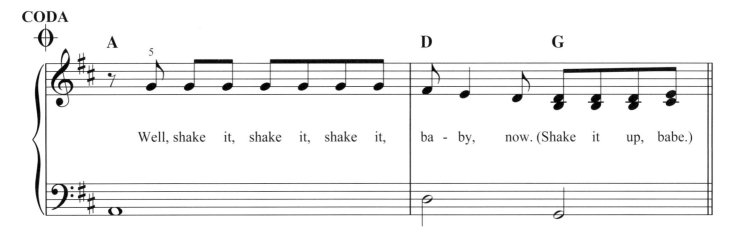

Well, shake it, shake it, shake it, ba - by, now. (Shake it up, babe.)

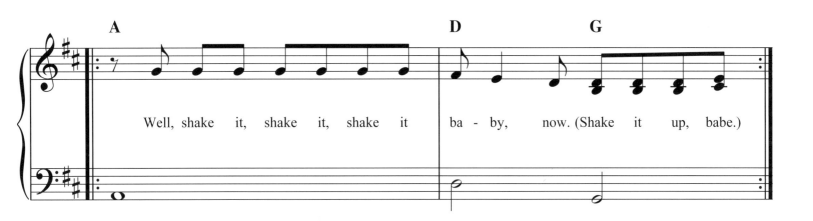

Well, shake it, shake it, shake it ba - by, now. (Shake it up, babe.)

Oo.   Ah,   ah,

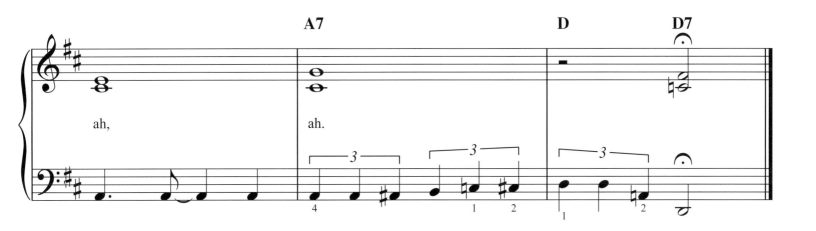

ah,   ah.

TICKET TO RIDE

Words and Music by JOHN LENNON
and PAUL McCARTNEY

Moderate Rock

I think I'm gon-na be sad, _____ I think it's to-day, _____
said that liv-ing with me _____ is bring-in' her down, _____

_____ yeah! The girl that's driv-ing me mad
_____ yeah! For she would nev-er be free _____

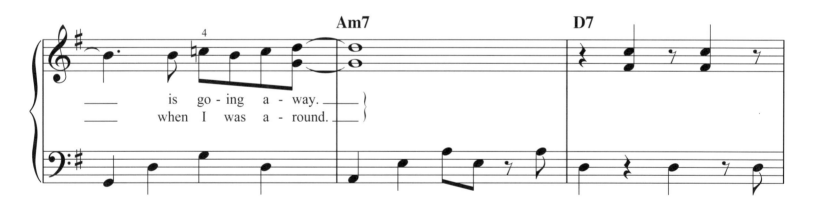

_____ is go-ing a-way. _____
when I was a-round. _____

Am7   **D7**

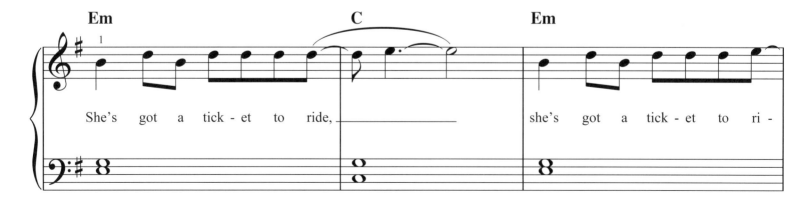

Em   **C**   **Em**

She's got a tick-et to ride, _____ she's got a tick-et to ri-

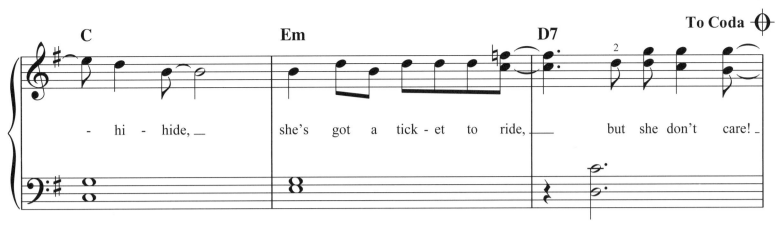

-hi -hide, __ she's got a tick-et to ride, __ but she don't care! __

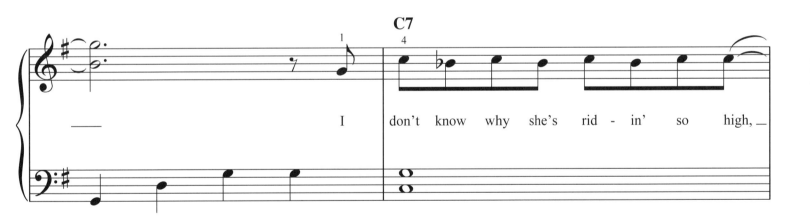

She

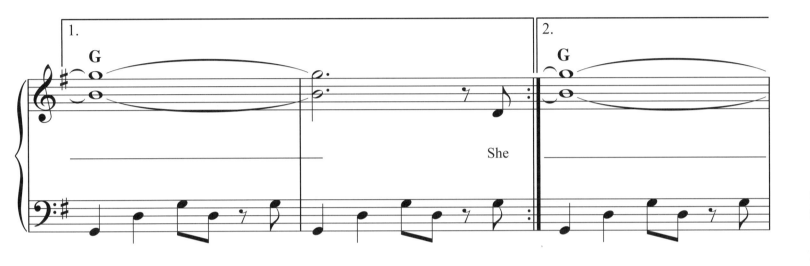

__ I don't know why she's rid-in' so high, __

she ought-a think twice, she ought-a do right by

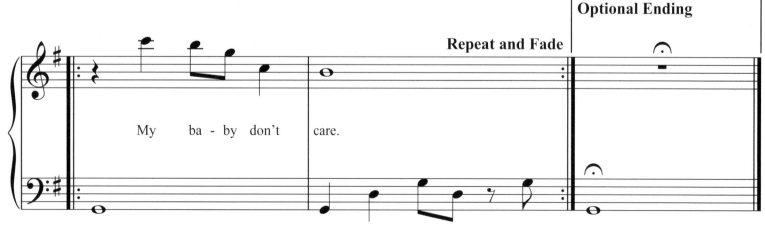

SHE'S A WOMAN

Words and Music by JOHN LENNON
and PAUL McCARTNEY

Fairly bright, with a strong back beat

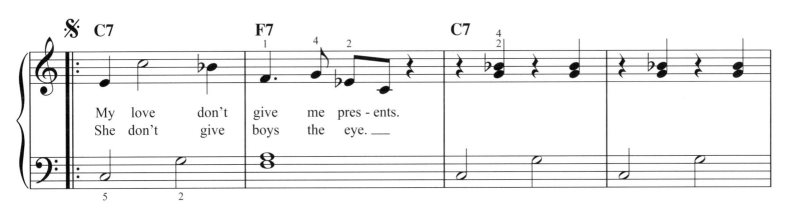

My love don't give me pres-ents.
She don't give boys the eye. ___

I know that she's no peas-ant.
She hates to see me cry. ___

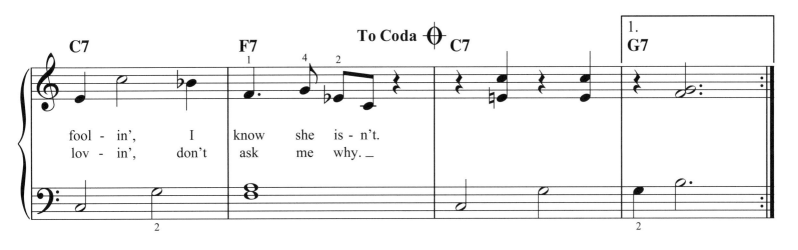

fool - in',   I   know   she   is - n't.
lov - in',   don't   ask   me   why. __

She's   a   wom - an   who   un - der - stands;

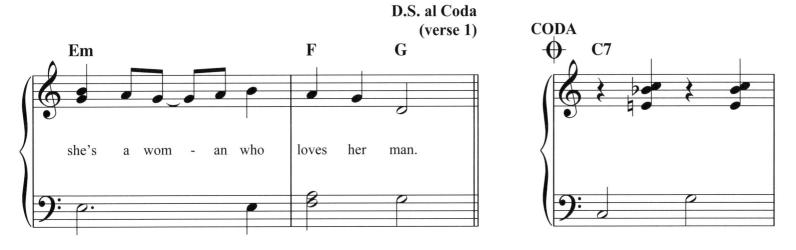

she's   a   wom - an   who   loves   her   man.

She's   a   wom - an. ____

DIZZY MISS LIZZIE

Words and Music by
LARRY WILLIAMS

Moderate Rock 'n' Roll

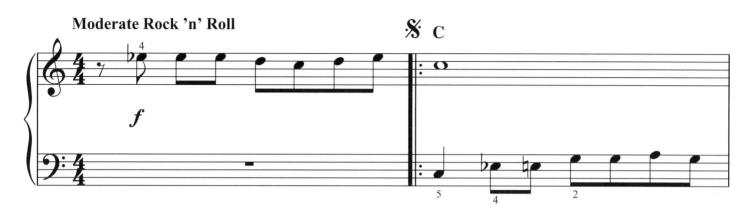

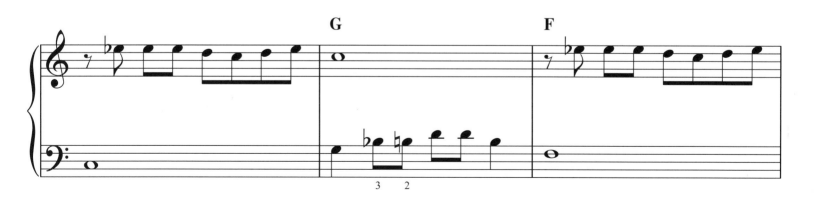

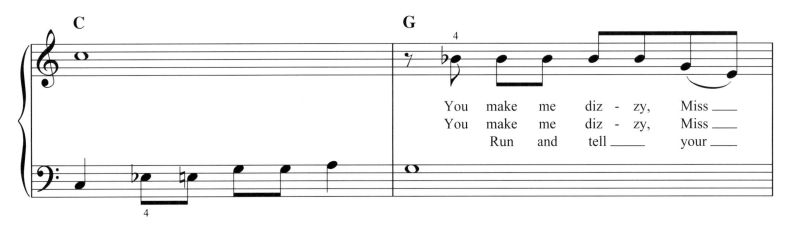

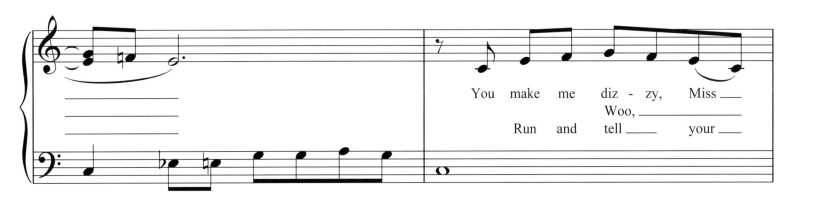

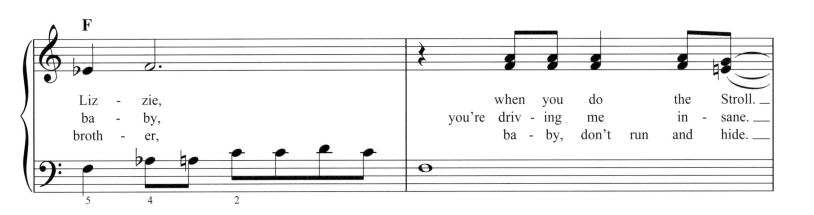

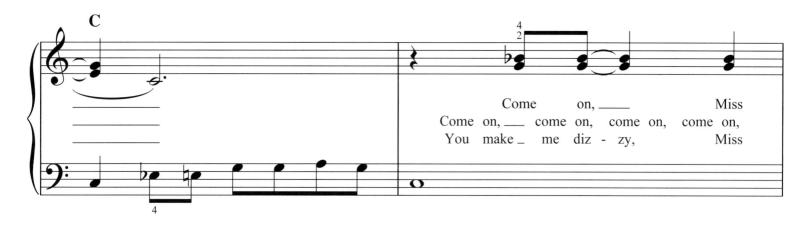

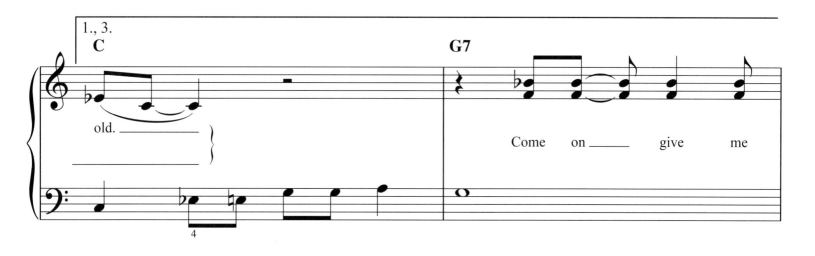

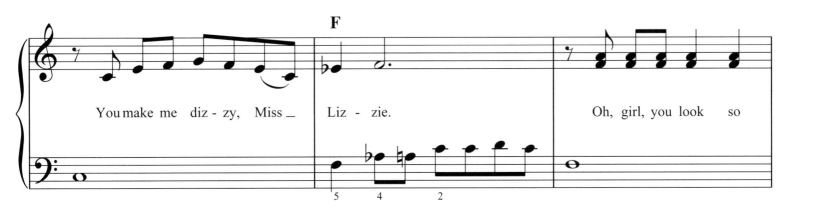

You make me diz - zy, Miss _ Liz - zie. Oh, girl, you look so

fine. _ Just a rock - in' and a - roll - in', _

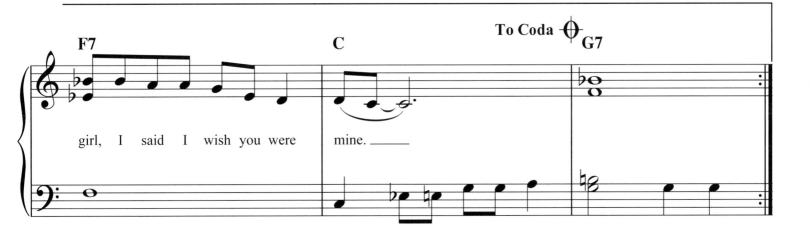

girl, I said I wish you were mine. _

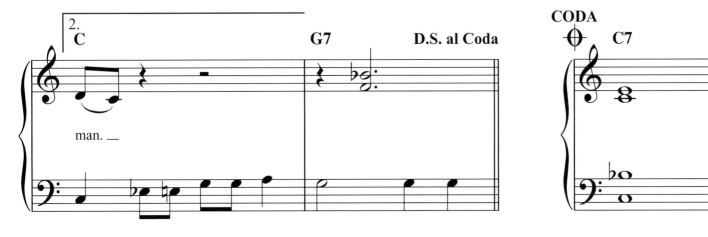

man. _

CAN'T BUY ME LOVE

Words and Music by JOHN LENNON
and PAUL McCARTNEY

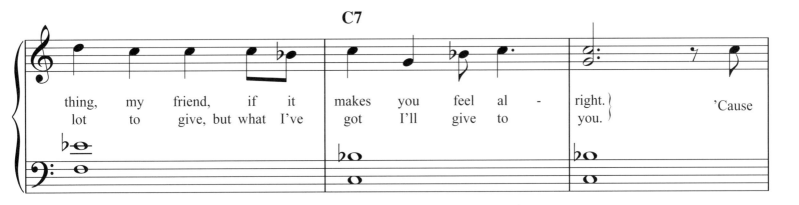

thing, my friend, if it makes you feel al - right.
lot to give, but what I've got I'll give to you.
'Cause

I don't care too much for mon - ey, mon - ey can't buy me

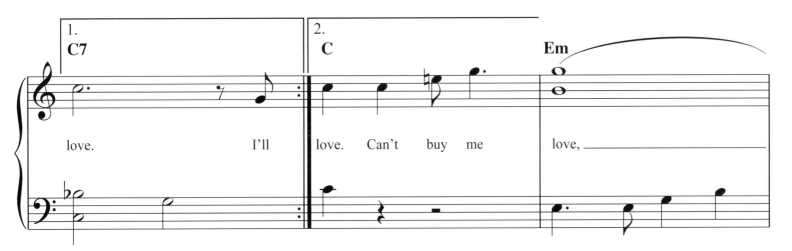

1.
love. I'll

2.
love. Can't buy me love, _____

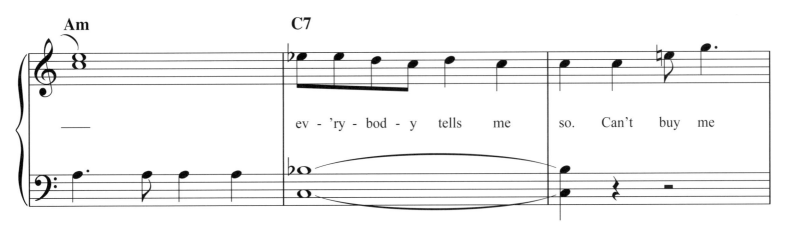

_____ ev - 'ry - bod - y tells me so. Can't buy me

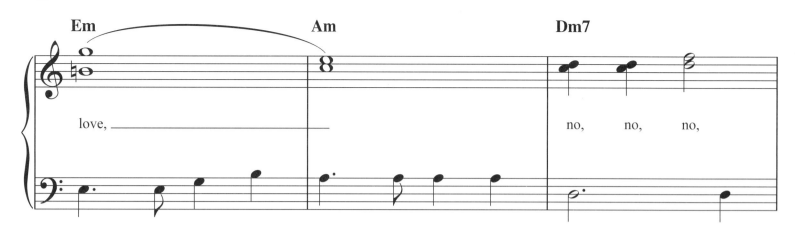

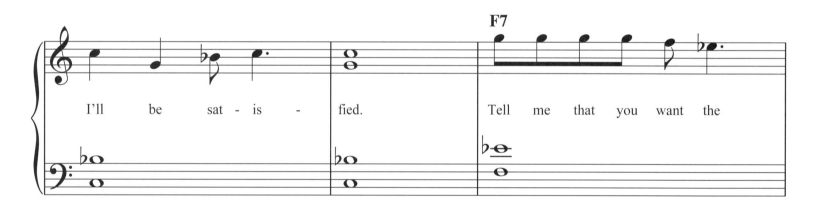

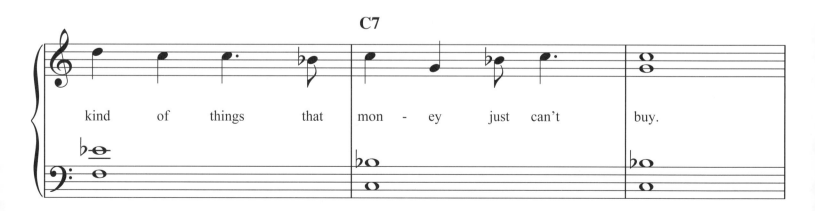

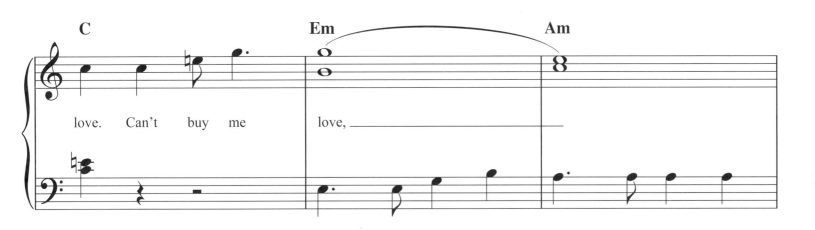

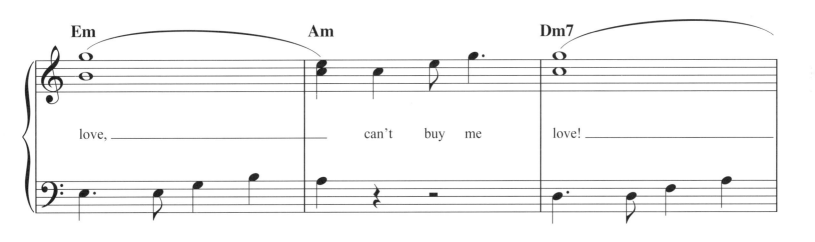

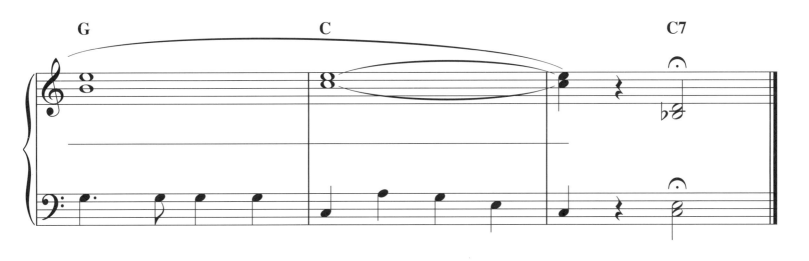

THINGS WE SAID TODAY

Words and Music by JOHN LENNON
and PAUL McCARTNEY

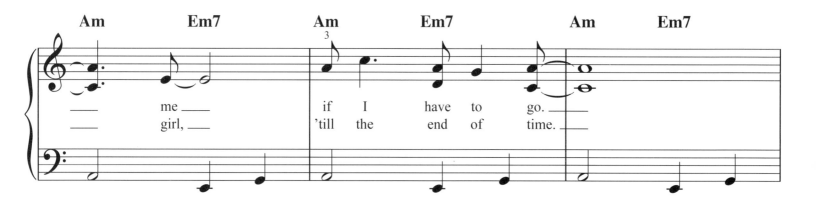

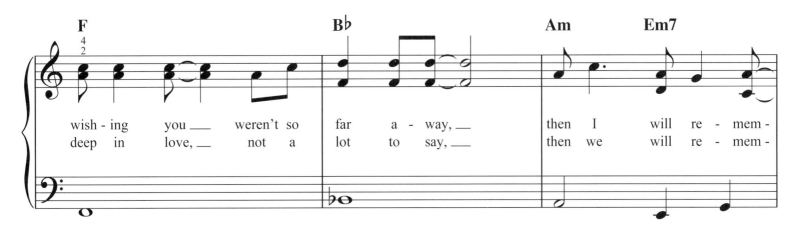

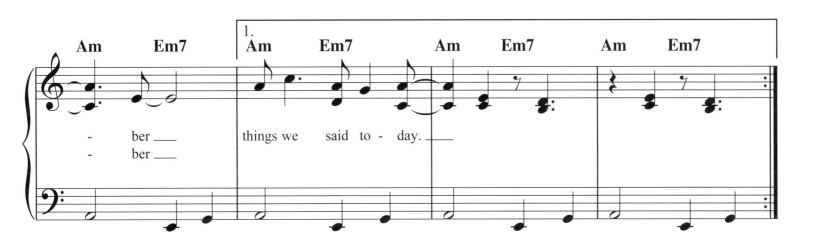

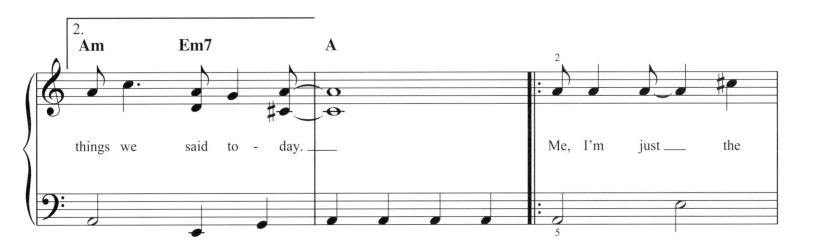

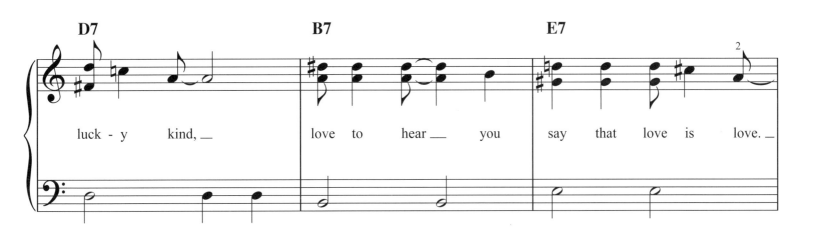

22

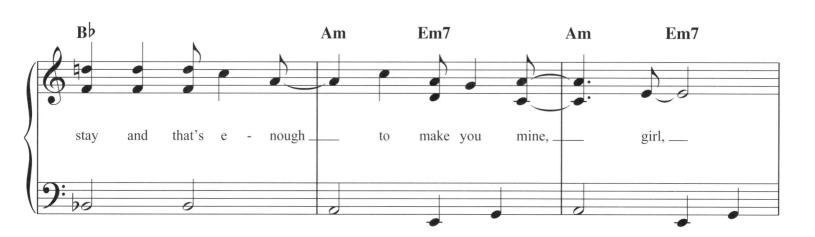

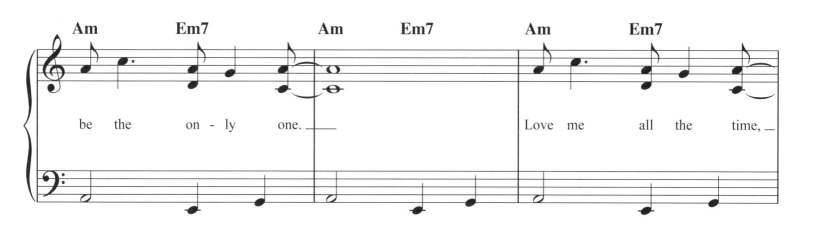

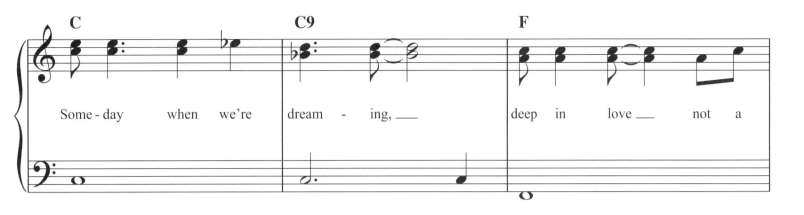

Some-day when we're dream - ing, ___ deep in love ___ not a

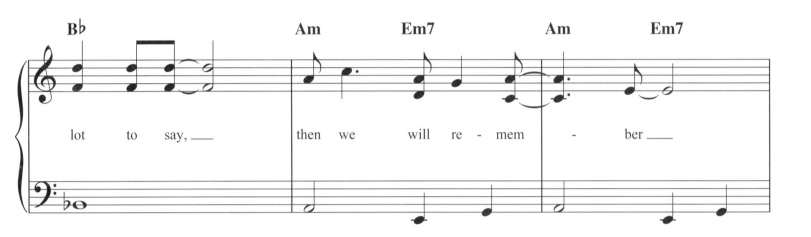

lot to say, ___ then we will re - mem - ber ___

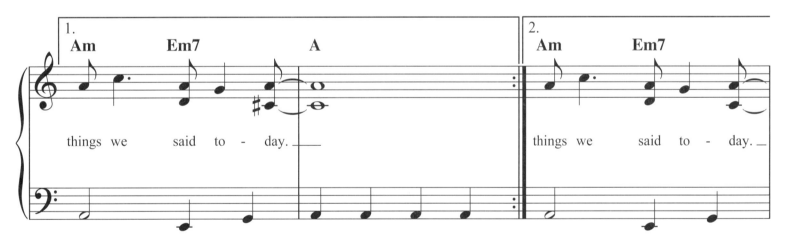

1.
things we said to - day. ___

2.
things we said to - day. __

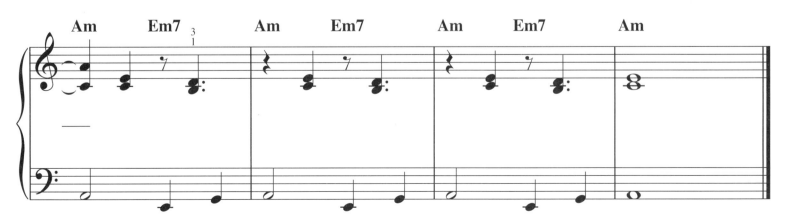

BOYS

Words and Music by LUTHER DIXON
and WES FARRELL

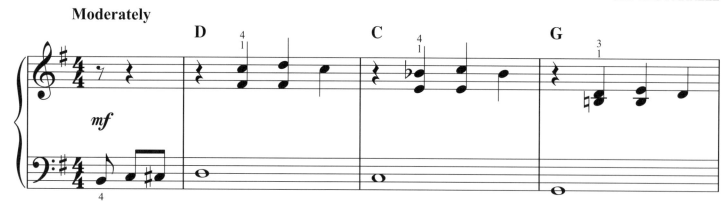

hey, _____   hey,   hey, _____

hey,   whoa,   she say you do. _____

Well, I talk a - bout   boys,

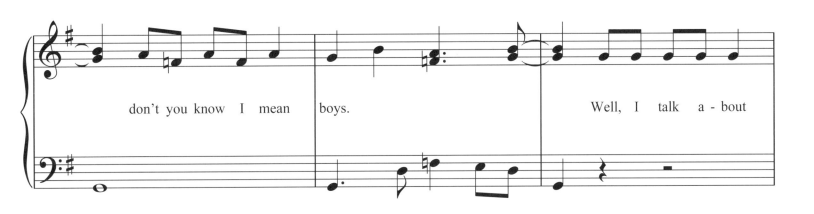

don't you know I mean   boys.   Well, I talk a - bout

boys, ___ ah boys.

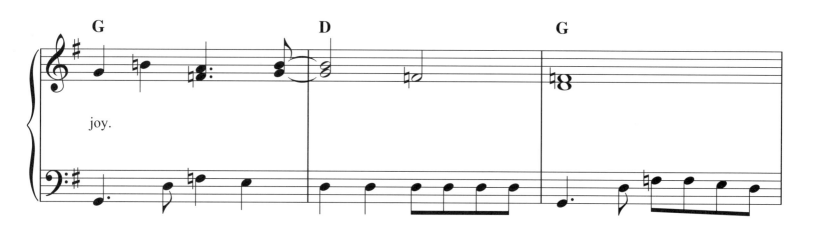

Well, I talk a - bout boys, now, what a bun - dle of

joy.

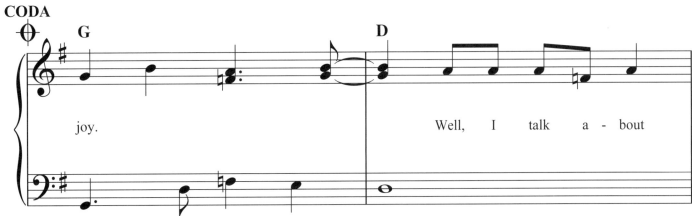

joy.

Well, I talk a - bout

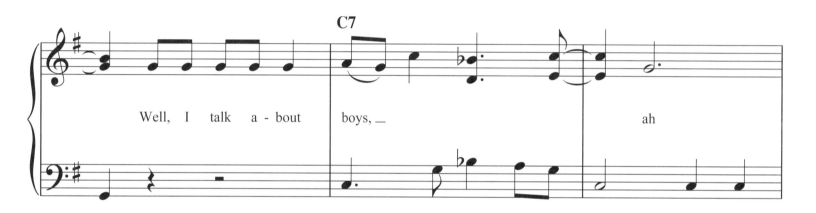

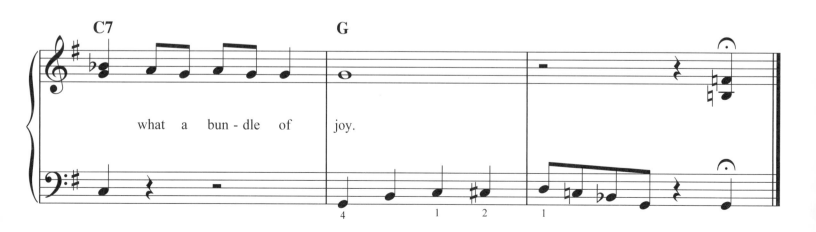

HELP!

Words and Music by JOHN LENNON
and PAUL McCARTNEY

Moderately, in 2

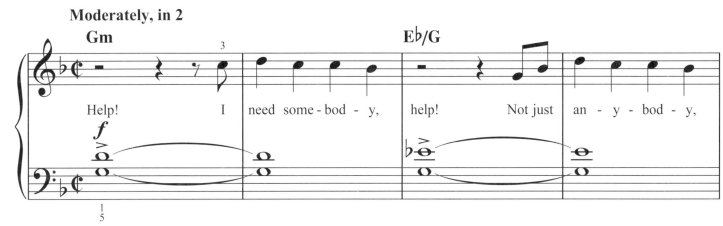

Help! I need some-bod-y, help! Not just an-y-bod-y,

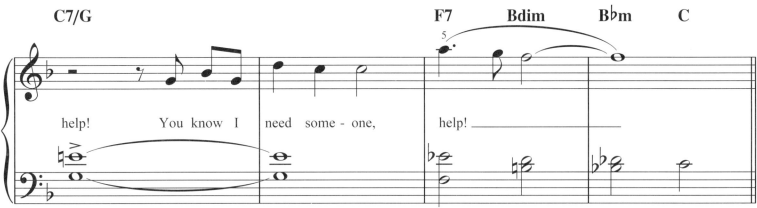

help! You know I need some-one, help!

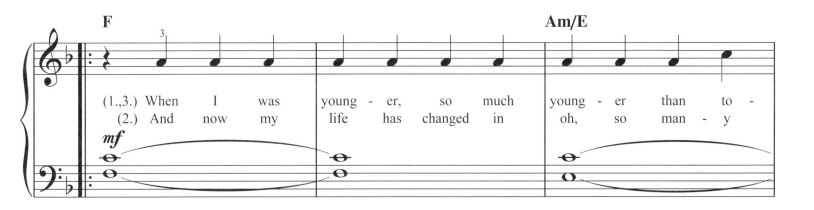

(1.,3.) When I was young-er, so much young-er than to-
(2.) And now my life has changed in oh, so man-y

day, I nev-er need-ed an-y-bod-y's
ways, my in-de-pen-dence seems to

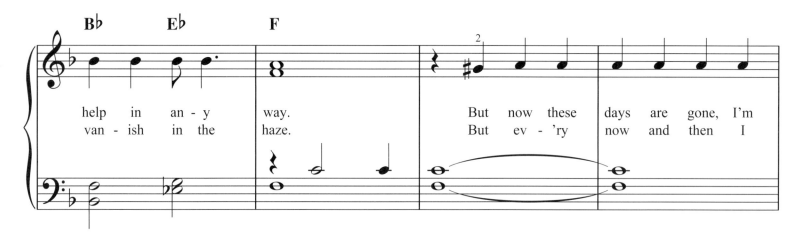

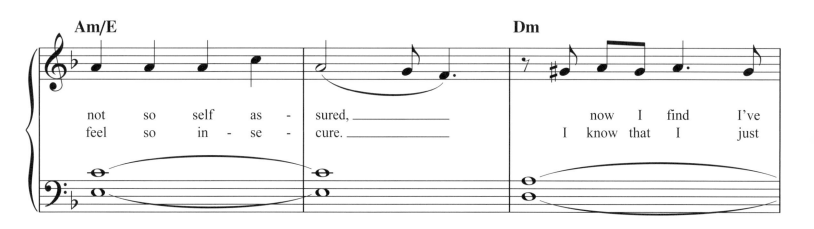

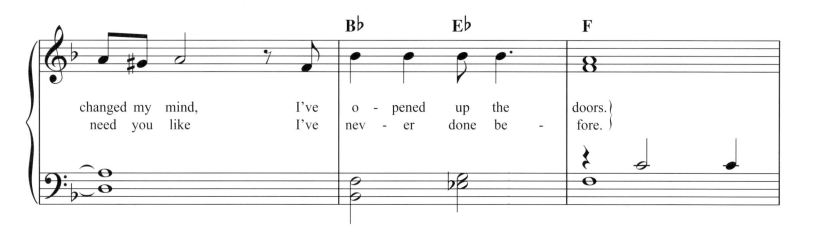

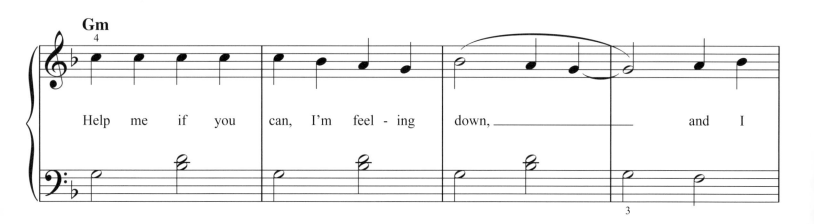

do ap - pre - ci - ate you be - ing 'round. _____

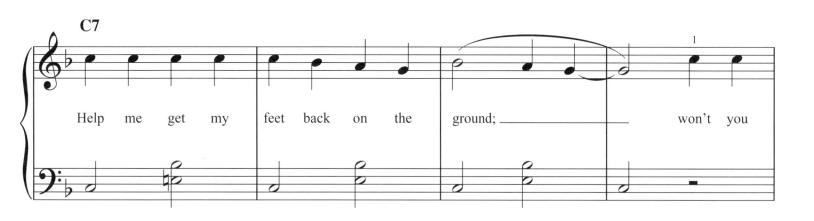

Help me get my feet back on the ground; _____ won't you

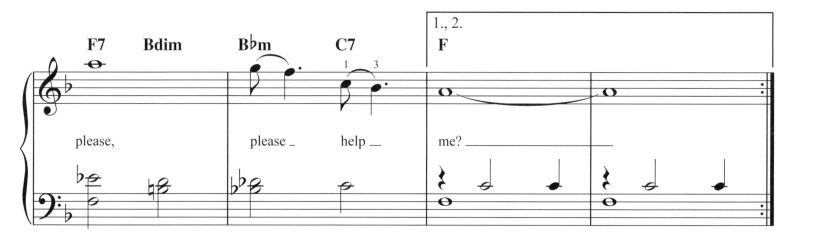

please, please _ help _ me? _____ me?

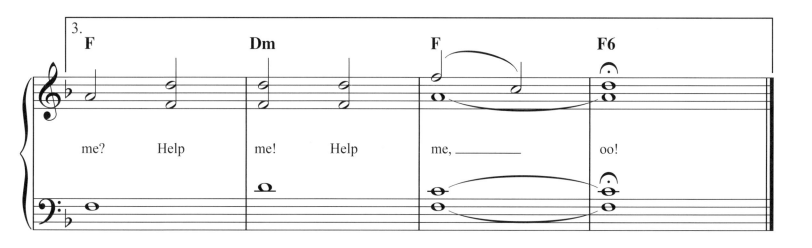

me? Help me! Help me, _____ oo!

A HARD DAY'S NIGHT

Words and Music by JOHN LENNON
and PAUL McCARTNEY

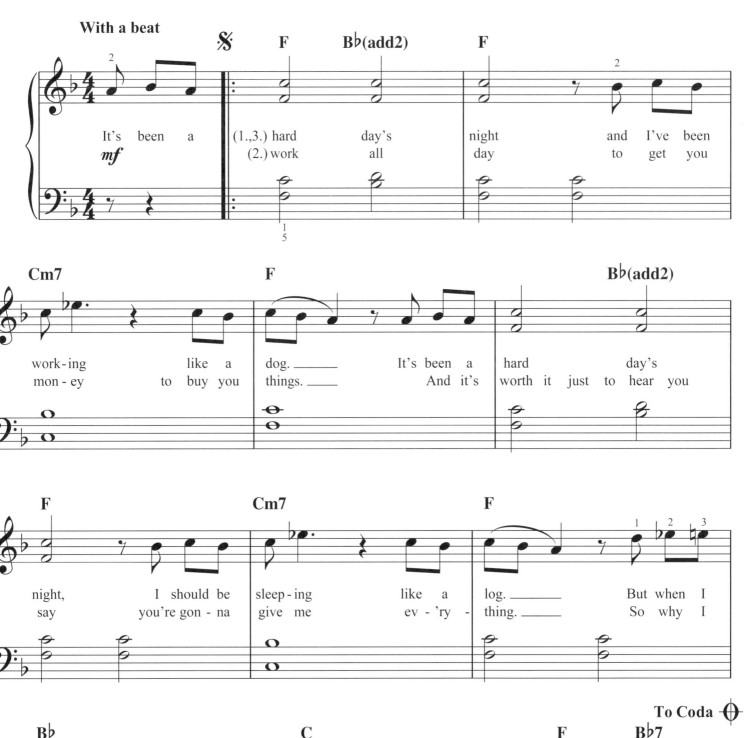

With a beat

It's been a (1.,3.) hard day's night and I've been
(2.) work all day to get you

work-ing like a dog. It's been a hard day's
mon-ey to buy you things. And it's worth it just to hear you

night, I should be sleep-ing like a log. But when I
say you're gon - na give me ev - 'ry - thing. So why I

To Coda

get home to you __ I find the thing that you do __ will make me feel al -
love to come home _ 'cause when I get you a - lone __ you know I'll be __ O.

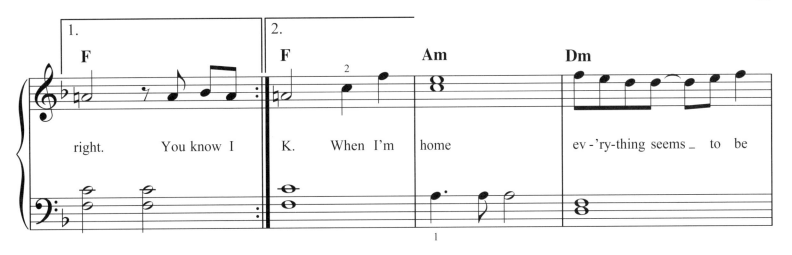

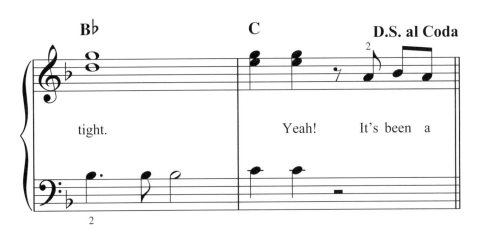
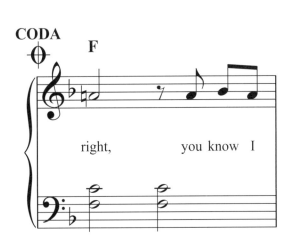

ALL MY LOVING

Words and Music by JOHN LENNON
and PAUL McCARTNEY

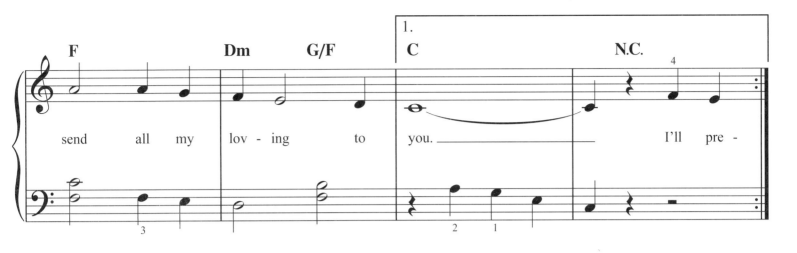

send all my lov - ing to you. I'll pre -

you. All my lov - ing, I will send to

you, all my lov - ing, dar - ling, I'll be

D.S. al Coda

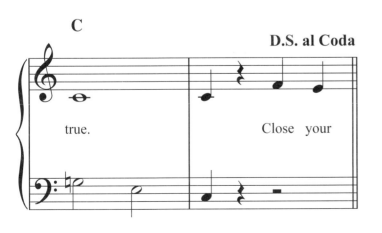

true. Close your

CODA

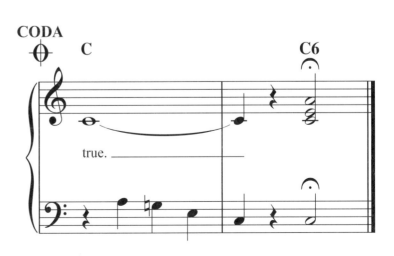

true.

SHE LOVES YOU

Words and Music by JOHN LENNON
and PAUL McCARTNEY

Brisk Rock tempo

She loves you yeah, yeah, yeah, she loves you, yeah,

yeah, yeah, she loves you, yeah, yeah, yeah, yeah.

You think you've lost your love? Well, I saw her yester-

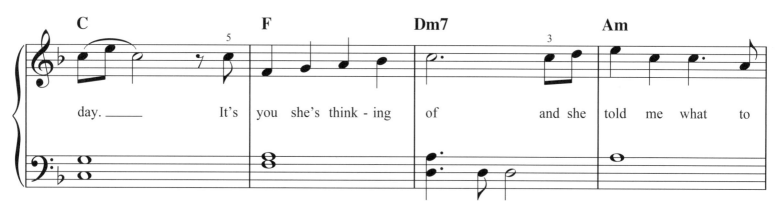

day. It's you she's think-ing of and she told me what to

say: _____ She says she loves you and you know that can't be

bad. Yes, she loves you and you know you should be

glad. _____ She said you hurt her so, she
know it's up to you, I

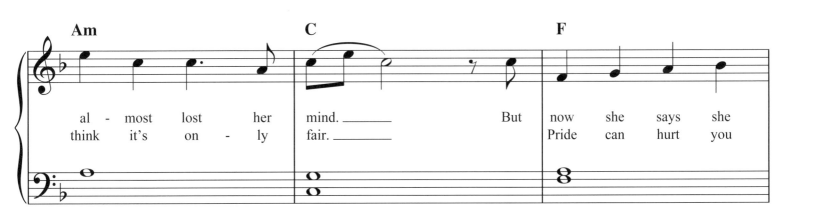

al - most lost her mind. _____ But now she says she
think it's on - ly fair. _____ Pride can hurt you

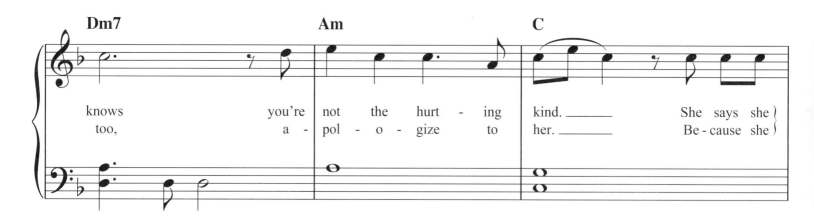

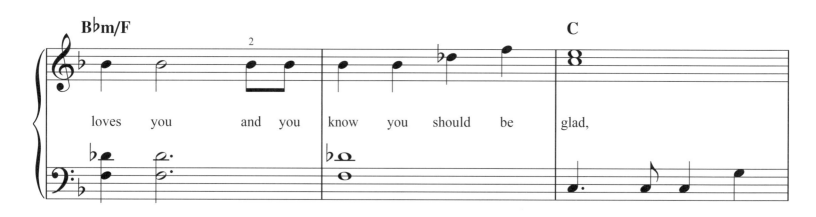

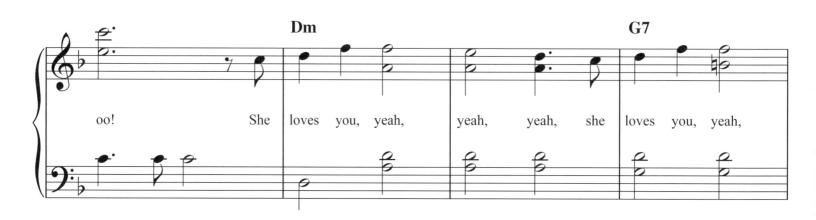

yeah, yeah. And with a love like that you know you should be

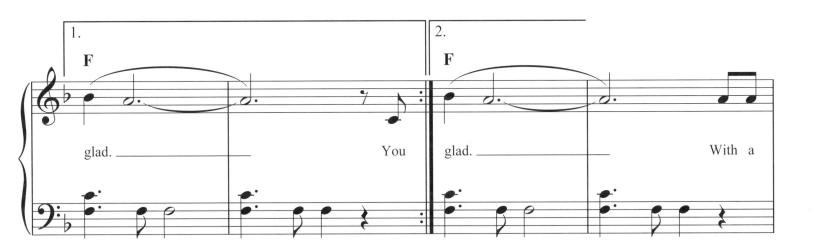

glad. _____ You glad. _____ With a

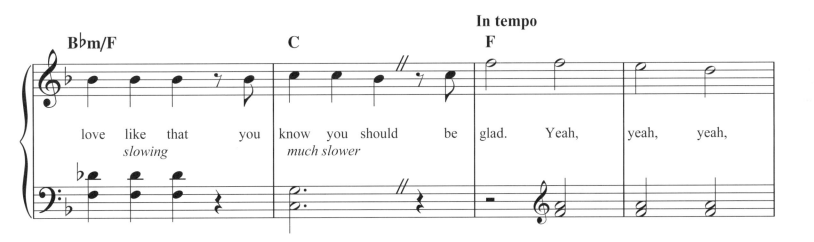

love like that you know you should be glad. Yeah, yeah, yeah,

slowing *much slower*

yeah, yeah, yeah, yeah, yeah, yeah, yeah!

LONG TALL SALLY

Words and Music by ENOTRIS JOHNSON,
RICHARD PENNIMAN and ROBERT BLACKWELL

Bright Rock

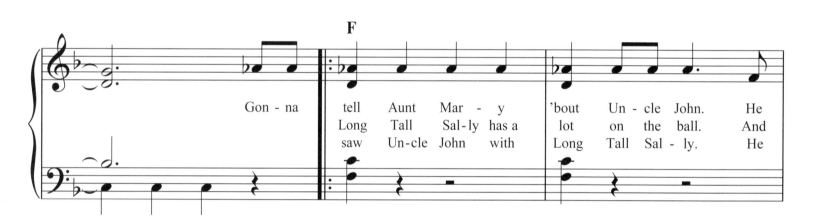

Gon - na tell Aunt Mar - y 'bout Un - cle John. He
Long Tall Sal - ly has a lot on the ball. And
saw Un - cle John with Long Tall Sal - ly. He

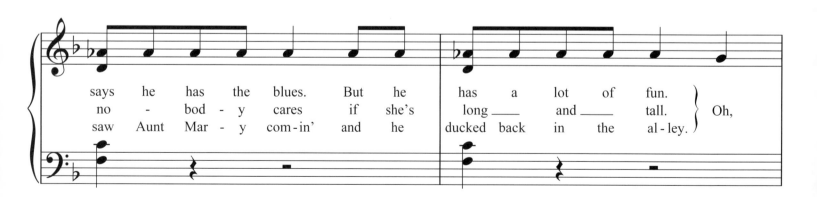

says he has the blues. But he has a lot of fun.
no - bod - y cares if she's long ___ and ___ tall. } Oh,
saw Aunt Mar - y com - in' and he ducked back in the al - ley.

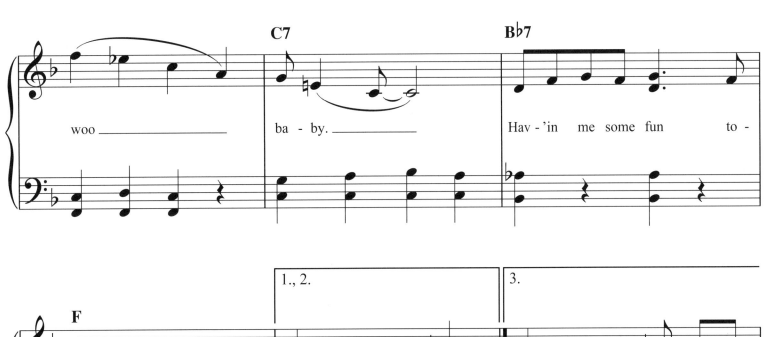

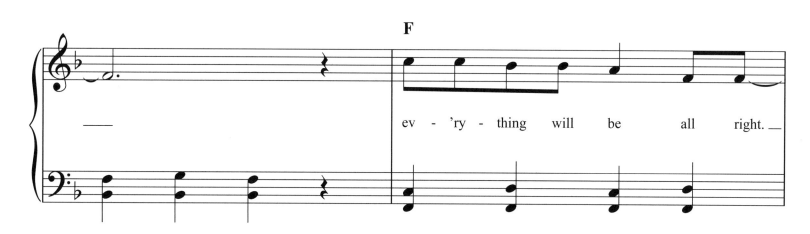

I WANT TO HOLD YOUR HAND

Words and Music by JOHN LENNON
and PAUL McCARTNEY

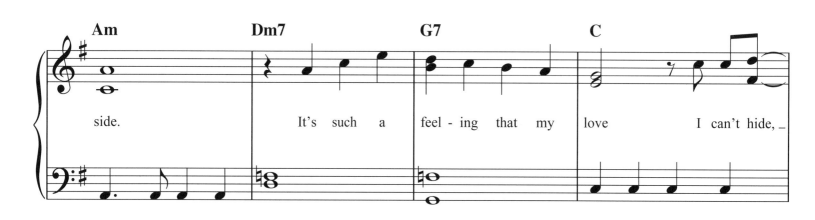

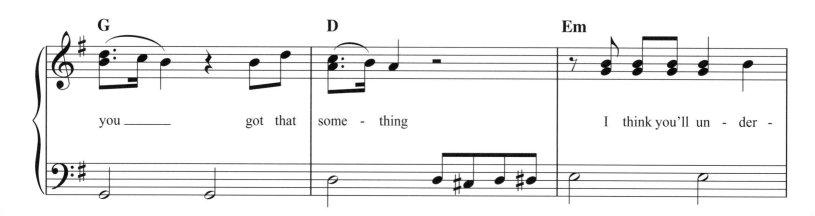

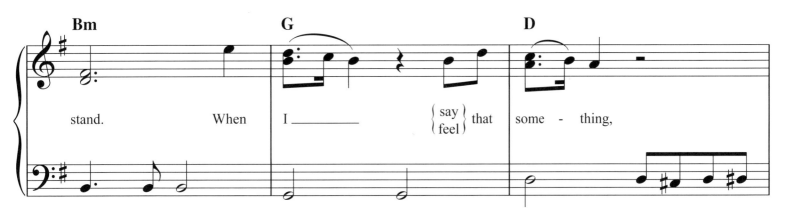

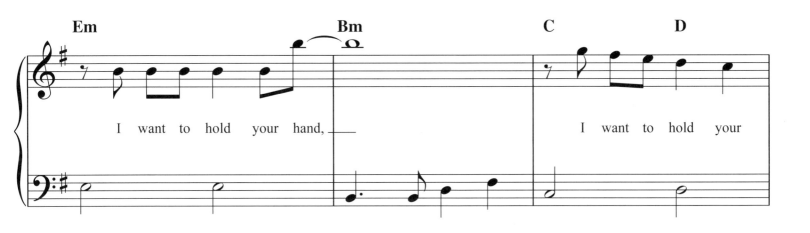

YOU CAN'T DO THAT

Words and Music by JOHN LENNON
and PAUL McCARTNEY

Moderately

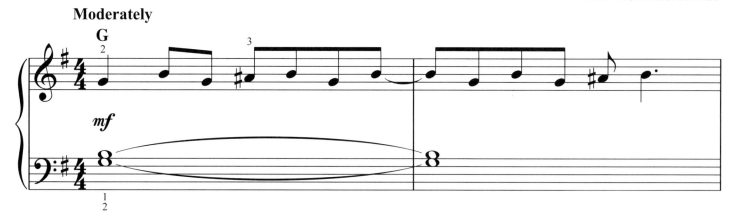

I got

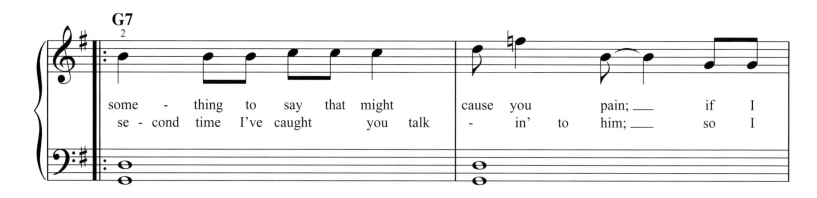

some - thing to say that might cause you pain; ___ if I
se - cond time I've caught you talk - in' to him; ___ so I

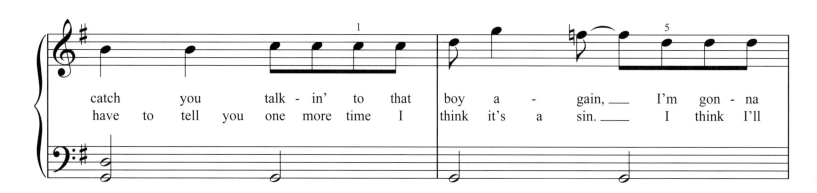

catch you talk - in' to that boy a - gain, ___ I'm gon - na
have to tell you one more time I think it's a sin. ___ I think I'll

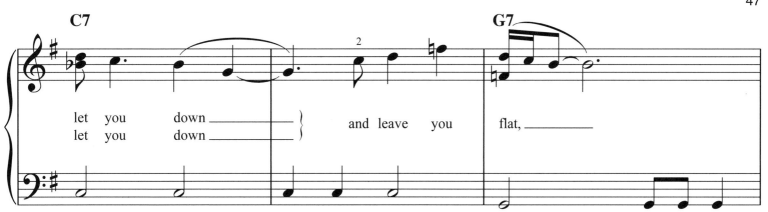

let you down _____ and leave you flat, _____
let you down _____

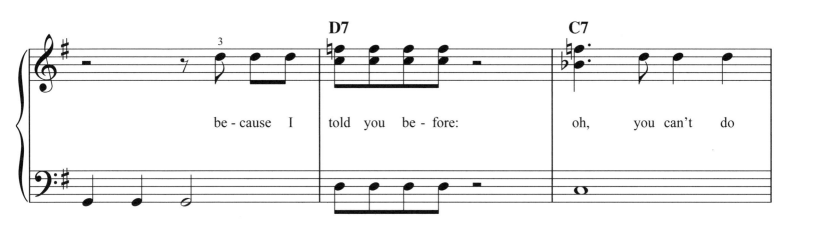

be - cause I told you be - fore: oh, you can't do

that. ____ Well, it's the Ev - 'ry - bod - y's

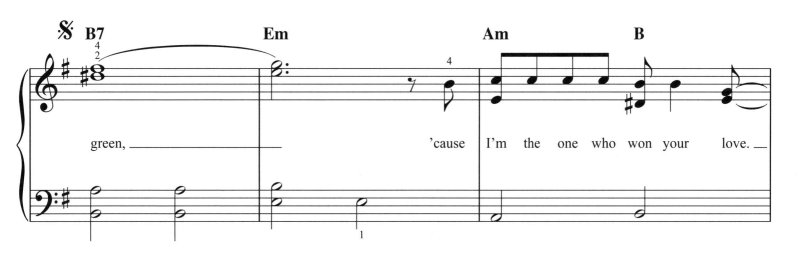

green, _____ 'cause I'm the one who won your love. ___

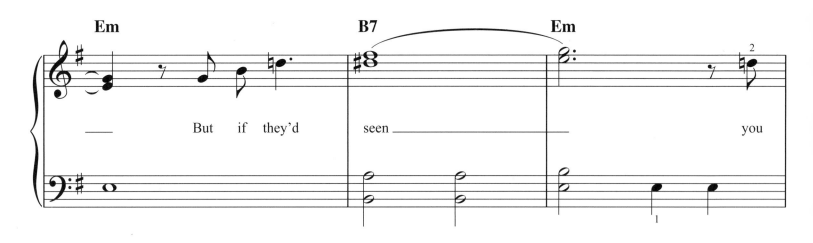

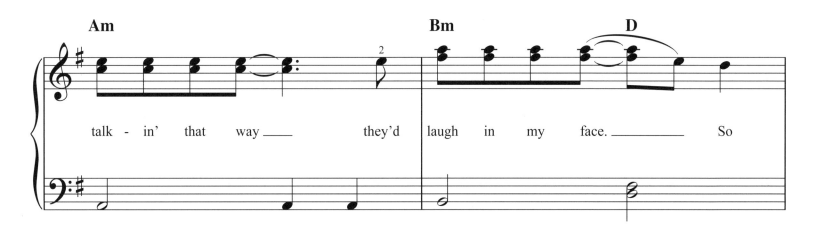

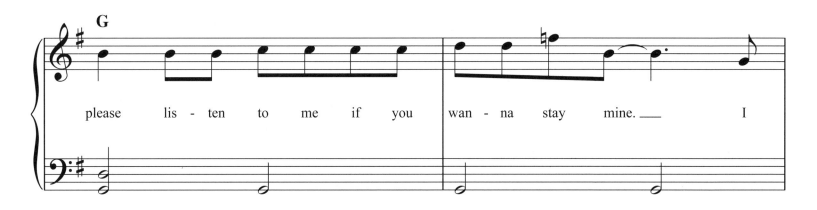

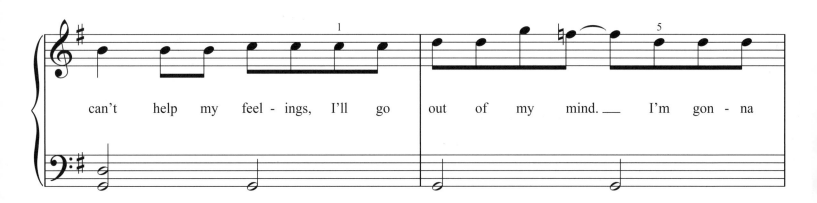

let you down _____ and leave you flat, _____

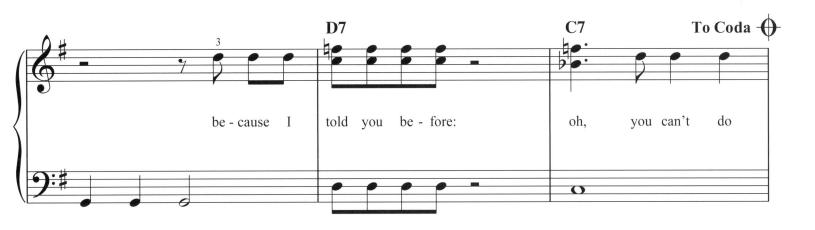

be - cause I told you be - fore: oh, you can't do

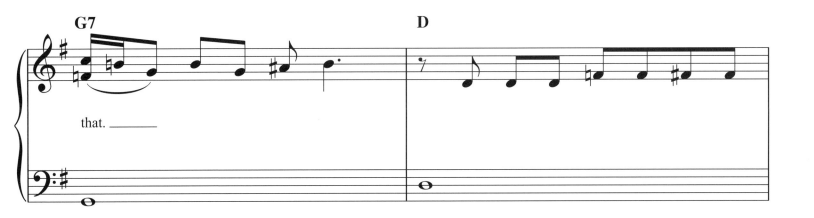

that. _____

BABY'S IN BLACK

Words and Music by JOHN LENNON
and PAUL McCARTNEY

Oh, how long will it take till she sees the mis-take she has

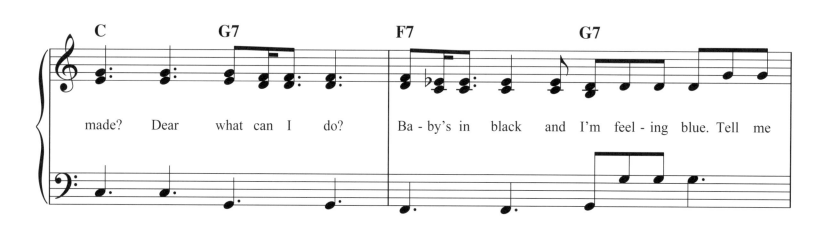

made? Dear what can I do? Ba-by's in black and I'm feel-ing blue. Tell me

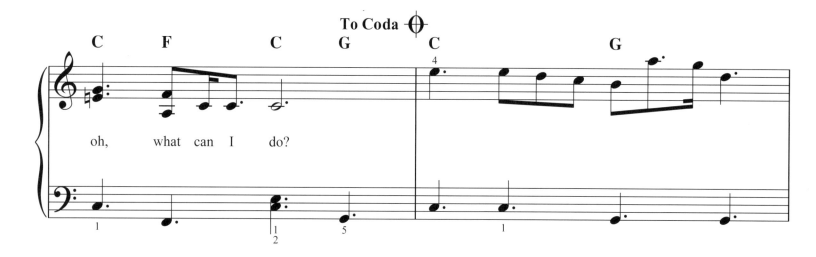

oh, what can I do?

CODA

She _____ thinks of him _____ and so she dress - es in black and

though he'll nev - er come back, she's dressed in black.

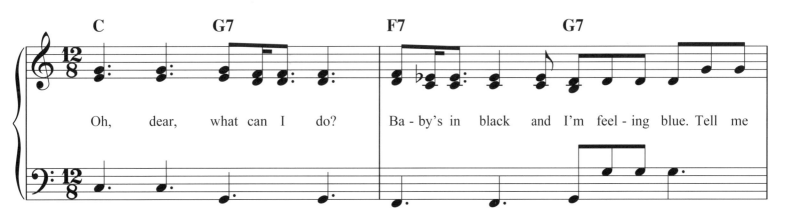

Oh, dear, what can I do? Ba - by's in black and I'm feel - ing blue. Tell me

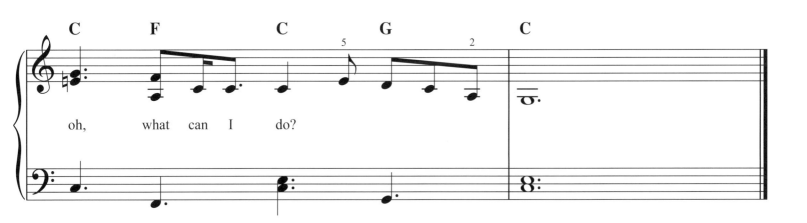

oh, what can I do?

EVERYBODY'S TRYING TO BE MY BABY

Words and Music by
CARL LEE PERKINS

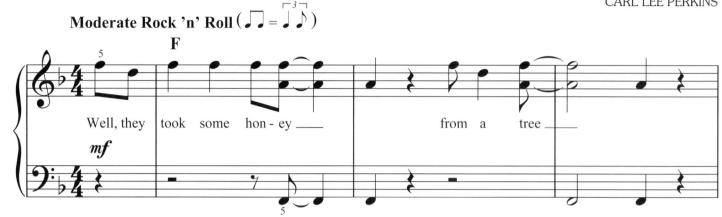

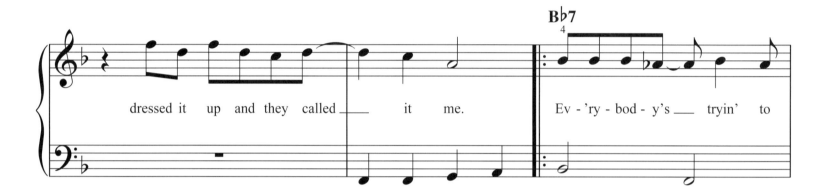

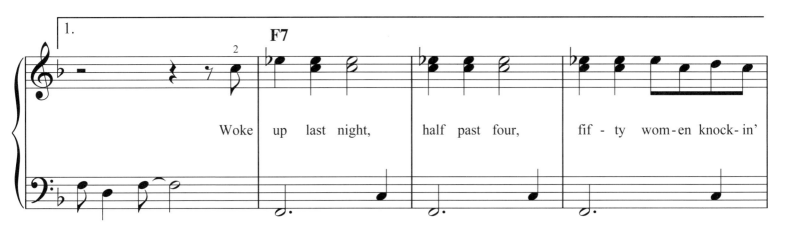

Woke up last night, half past four, fif - ty wom-en knock-in'

on my door.

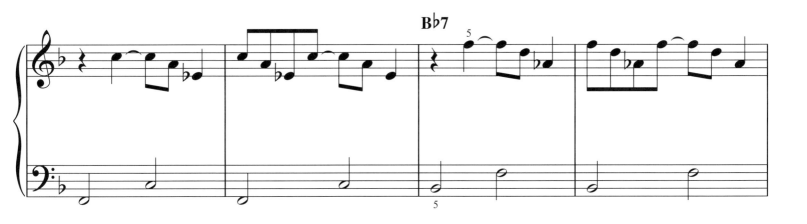

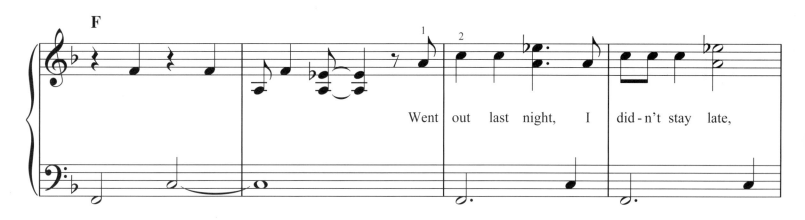

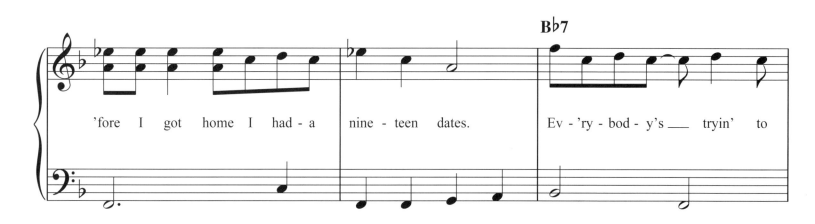

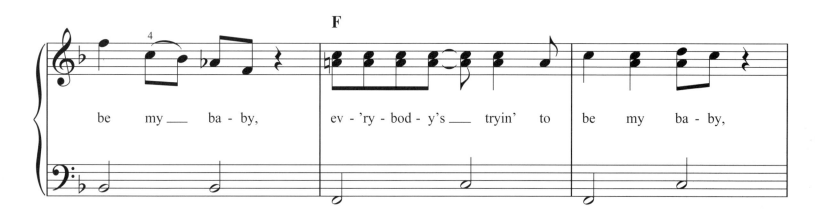

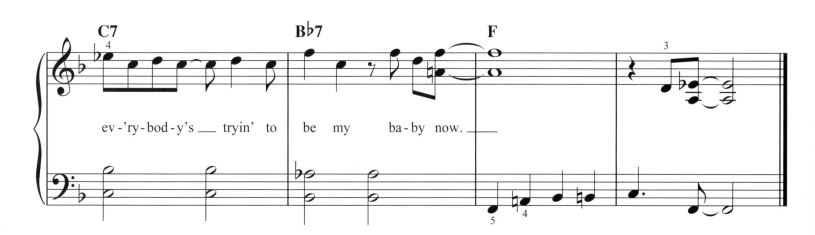